Nevertheless, I Am Whole

Nevertheless, I Am Whole

a journey of starting over and over

Niaje Adah

Nevertheless, I am whole copyright © 2021 Niaje Adah

ISBN: 978-0-578-84207-3

All rights reserved. Printed in The United States of America. No part of this book may be used or reproduced in any matter whatsoever without written permission except in the case of reprints in the context of reviews.

*For my Mother, Mama Niko, the miracle, the survivor.
You showed me how to continually push through.
You are the embodiment of perseverance.*

*For my Baba, Michael Bernard Beckwith-
You never gave up on me. Love- eternal.*

*To my Ancestors, my big sister Nairobi Dimitra
and Momma Joyce Young.*

*And Last, to the Pisces, a soulmate, who almost broke
me, yet made me realize exactly why I wrote this book.*

For Myself.
*With an open heart, I give all thanks to the creator.
What a journey. amen. ase.*

May 23rd 2016, my world changed forever, the day I was diagnosed with cancer. I had been waiting for my results for over 2 weeks. The day had finally come. I'll never forget my doctor telling me my tumor was cancerous. I'd had ongoing minor gynecological issues before, so naturally I thought this would be small. Remove the tumor, get on with my life. But this was different. Talk of chemotherapy and radiation were thrown quickly at me. I was in a blur... I couldn't process all of this, I couldn't focus. I began to sweat and had to kneel down to prevent passing out. I walked out of the hospital alone. I didn't know who to call. I didn't know how to tell my mother, and my boyfriend, had broken up with me literally days prior. I walked from 18th street all the way up to 135th street Harlem in a daze. A week later I had surgery followed by chemotherapy and radiation. Life was coming at me fast. I had no time to process any of it. I was thrown into a world which seemed to keep getting worse and worse. Oh yea, I was diagnosed with stage IV cancer, and eventually given just 15 months to live. How do you digest such information?

That is where this journey began. Now four years later, I am still fighting to maintain my health, sanity, and a sense of normalcy. I am still fighting for my heart to heal. Above all else, I am still standing. I give thanks for my superpowers of strength and vulnerability. Putting pen to paper has saved my life. I have literally written through, and shared my entire journey. Through this process I started to see how other people could relate to my story. Whether fighting a disease or not, the human experience was shared. I started to see that everyone is fighting some sort of battle. Everyone has felt pain, heartache, loneliness and confusion in some manner. I think everyone has questioned the Creator at some point, and still we make it through, hope and joy trickle in and we continue on our paths.

I didn't want to write another "cancer story", another "Lifetime docu-pic" about nearly dying and coming out victorious. Nah, that wasn't it. This is not the typical testimony.

More so, daily snippets of how I'm getting through, because honestly I'm still going through it.

My story is about so much more than cancer. It's about heartbreak, self worth, and starting over and over again. This is survival that I've wrapped into a collection of words, born from the deep feelings I've felt over the past four years. A journey of Self discovery...mine.

So yes, this book is not only for those who are fighting disease or who have fought disease. This is for those who have hit rock bottom, shattered into pieces, and despite it all put the pieces back together. This is for those who have put themselves back together and then broke into pieces once again. This is for the ones whose many broken pieces no longer fit like they once did, who come to the light and realize their broken pieces will not ever fit back into their original state. They are to be rebuilt into something new. Reborn into something greater. This is for those who despite everything that tried to break them apart for good, realized nevertheless, they are still whole.

Stage I.
Diagnosed & Dealing with it all.

Faith

For the moment

She is broken

And that is ok

She will be whole again.

Good Mourning

I woke up

And didn't recognize myself in the mirror

All i could see was cancer

All i could feel was heartbreak

All i could hear was " I love you but i'm no longer IN love with you"

All i wanted was to disappear

Joke

Going through cancer & a breakup feels like being cut by a double edged sword.

What did I do to deserve this?

God give me the strength.

Paul-
Journal entry 9.20.16

I remember the old me. I can dream about the future me. The current me is what I am trying to deal with. Yes I believe true beauty is on the inside but I am a woman and I am human. My physical form is testing my strength. I am beyond thin, I have no hair, my skin is pale, and I have dark discoloration on my face. I try to look in the mirror every morning and say "I am beautiful", but on this day I didn't feel it. I couldn't see it. Times like these I wish I had a lover to look me in my eyes, give me a kiss and tell me I'm beautiful. Not because I am weak or need validation from someone else, but because that type of love heals and feels damn good.

A week ago I was sitting in a blood lab and I started a conversation with a man named Paul. Paul was in pain, you could see it all over his face. Paul's wife was battling stomach cancer. He asked me about my cancer and my relationship status. He dropped gems about love and patience, about how he holds his wife and kisses her as if they just met. How loving someone with cancer is such a hard test. How he wouldn't wish that pain on anyone, but he knew his love helped her immensely. It helps heal her and gives her a little bit more life each day. Their story was heartbreaking but beautiful. That is not my story, I am being tested as well and will come to my own understanding of this journey eventually. This goes to say I appreciate and I am beyond eternally grateful for what love I do receive on a daily basis. In no way am I discrediting the love I receive from family and friends, but if a girl can be real, some days I just want to spoon and cry in my lover's arms. To feel protected and adored. Especially days like today, when I look in the mirror and can't see the beauty I know is hiding somewhere inside. The beauty that has always been there.

Pain

hits like bricks

and

sticks like honey.

Vulnerability

I am stripped down to a shell of my old self. Nothing left but a little room to build something new upon. Blessed to see another day. Faith that I'll see tomorrow. As I lay in bed, I realize how hard my nights are. My body begins to rest but my mind races like Nascar. I toss and turn, letting out tears until I eventually fall asleep. True it gets easier day by day; but pain hits like bricks and sticks like honey. I remind myself that this is a temporary state. This is a temporary Niaje. All of this. I close my eyes and see images of the past. I tear up again… I have a conversation with the Moon, God hears me . My prayers are heard. I close my eyes again and meditate. My meditation will lead me to the dreamworld. I will rise again to a new day. Goodnight

Support

I got tucked into bed by the Moon last night.

Woke up to the Sun kissing my forehead.

Reflection.

Today is one of those days I'm not proud of, today I am no warrior. I am tired and I am hurt. I woke up filled with anxiety about everything. Future surgeries, endings, new beginnings, everything. My body is in constant pain. I am overwhelmed with emotion and I've started taking it out on the people I love. I have lost my beauty, my confidence, and my independence. I live with the possibility of losing my life. This is all too much, so today I will allow myself to cry, scream and be scared. Tomorrow will be a new day. My whole life has changed in 8 months, and it all weighs so heavy I feel like I can't breathe. I want to be complete. I want to know, not just believe, that I am loved and protected by a higher force. I question God at times but I know God never fails. I have to have patience and acceptance for whatever is in store for me. Today I am allowing myself to feel it all.

Real

Let it out.

Feel all the feels

Don't mind other's opinions

Transparency only bothers those afraid of

Themselves.

Initiation

This is NOT depression. This is living with cancer. This is missing my loved ones across the country. This is being tired. This is mal-nutrition. This is body pain. This is uncertainty. This is fear. This is a release. Day one of a new chemo drug and I'm tired. I'm tired of all of this. I am weak today. I am nobody's inspiration today. I continue to fight through my pain, my sadness and my tears. I have not given up. No, but I'm tired. I just want to be held. I just want to be ok at this moment. God strengthens me, but even the strongest people cry and need reassurance at times. Today is that day. Tomorrow will be different. I must remember this is my initiation into glory. It ain't easy.

Temporary

This is all temporary. Wounds are destined to heal. Scars both physical and mental will be worn like medals of honor one day. I am becoming more powerful of a woman than I could ever have imagined

Affirmation : I will rise again

| **Sip**

She drank a cup of tea to warm her body and heal her soul.

She adds honey to sweeten the bitterness of the day.

For now, she is at peace.

A cup of Sweet Honey Tea - With Lemon, Ginger & Thyme

Ingredients

- 1/2 lemon sliced
- 1 inch ginger root peeled & sliced
- 2 to 3 sprigs of Thyme
- 1 ½ cup water
- Honey (as much as you damn please)

Instructions

1. Place lemon slices, ginger, thyme and water in small pot
2. Let it come to a boil then turn off heat and cover
3. Steep for 10 to 15 minutes then strain into cup
4. Add honey.
5. Enjoy!

Warrior

And then

There are days the weight of the shield

is too heavy to carry.

In my solitude

Journal entry - 2.2017

Did you know they call cancer the lonely disease?

I'm not sure what I thought my experience would be, BUT shit got real, real fast. In the beginning I was terrified, I didn't know what was to come. I held on to faith and hope like a security blanket. I was covered, so I thought. I had soooo many people around. Visitors, calls, texts, flowers, gifts... then, slowly, all that began to fade away. The visits lessened. My phone stopped ringing, no more weekly flowers or gifts. Reality hit. I was no longer the loved one just diagnosed with cancer, but simply Niaje w/ cancer. That's how it felt. Funny thing is, I never thought my battle would be this long. It went from what looked like an easy tumor removal, to cancer cells throughout my body, and a life expectancy of 15 months. I noticed how people seemed to hold onto me like a fond memory.

On social media, everyone knew me and was my "friend". At one point I was a trending topic on my insta feed. Cancer isn't trendy though, it's serious, and unlike most trends it doesn't just fade away. So what now? I'm still alive.

By the grace of God I am surviving. I appreciate those who choose to continue to support and love me now as if it were still day one. I know it's not easy, I do. It's not easy watching your loved one on such a roller coaster ride. To watch me deteriorate, get stronger just to get knocked back down, again. You sacrifice your time and energy. Thank you for not loving me from a distance physically and emotionally. For not allowing fear to get in the way. I know it's scary, I'm scared as shit, but without support I would not survive. I canceled a lot of plans. I can't do all the things I use to do but you still see me. At times I tell myself I deserve distance because I myself am not the best friend or family member I can be at this moment, but you still show me love. Love is a verb. Without action the word means nothing. It's damn near two years in and I still need the same amount of support I needed on day one. I'm not Wonder Woman. I'm not just a muse for motivation and inspiration for endeavors. I am still Niaje. Living this human experience with one hell of a load on my shoulders. I may not be the same person I was two years ago, but I am still here. To the ones who still see that, you are appreciated.

Los Colores

Some days I'm Blue as Denim;

And that's ok,

because Most days

I'm bright like the Sun.

Troubled Weather

The sun always shines after the storm.

In the meantime, do not reside in fear.

Feel it.

let it move right through and out of you.

The best thing to do during a storm is to reflect, strategize and

plan for the future.

Tap all the way in and take care of any unresolved issues you have been holding onto.

Life can change in an instant. Be prepared. Allow the weather to move through you but never forget,

All storms pass.

Truth

Everyday I try to tell myself how brave and how much of a warrior I am.

Some days I believe,

Some days I don't.

Everyday is a fight.

Nevertheless, i am here

Smiles & Frowns
Journal entry - 10.2016

Good Morning my loves,

Today marks my seventh day in the hospital. My body has hit what they call the cancer wall. Low blood counts, extreme fatigue, intestinal issues, passing out, and now being force fed through a tube that goes through my nose into my stomach. I have had multiple blood transfusions, two heart injections, stomach fluid extractions, MRI's and x-rays and numerous tests ran on me. Nothing new is happening; it's all maintaining this body that is currently going through hell! People tend to get upset with me when I talk about my pain, as if my mindset is all wrong, as if I am focused on the negative and not the positive. I don't know, but I think I'm doing a pretty damn good job! I've been in this hospital 7 days and I have worn both smiles and frowns. I have laughed and cried and I have survived. I have not given up. My spirituality and faith, no matter how down I get, is getting me through this. To be spiritual is not to be positive all the time. It's to be aware. Aware of the negative and the positive. From there you make choices.

If I were to dwell and sulk in the negative, I never would have made it this far, trust me. Until one can walk in another's shoes all we can do is show support. Advice is limited to opinion in situations like these.

Metamorphosis

They fail to mention

how painful The process is

to transform and emerge

as the butterfly

I Am here
Journal entry - 2.2017

I could write a whole lot about what has been happening to me these past couple of weeks. Being hospitalized for this long is not easy. The one truth I know is, I am still here. I am still breathing. I am still fighting. There were nights where I almost did not make it. Heart issues, fevers, blood loss, infections, surgeries, an induced coma. This is not a nightmarish dream I have yet to wake up from, this is my reality. A sense of peace has come over me... whatever happens will happen.. and that's all I need. I am here. I am alive. I am writing and sharing my story with you all again. I am blessed to have people who love me. The ones who have sacrificed their time to reach out, call, visit and pray for me. I thank you all. I need not focus on those who are missing. I have held on to expectations long enough. I can not put any more energy into why someone may or may not love me, or want to be here for me anymore. It's their loss. I am beautiful, I am blessed. I am a living breathing miracle! I know I have to fight harder than the average person, still I fight! I am not positive every damn day. That's not realistic. But every day I wake up and do my best. I do my best when they tell me my heart is dying... I do my best when they give me a 15 month life expectancy. I do my best when my tumors have clustered and my immune system is failing. I will do my best!! I am proud of the way I have fought this battle. I am proud of my inner warrior. I still believe my miracle is coming but for now today is all that matters, this is the moment. Let's make the best of it.

Niaje Adah

Still, i keep fighting

I am at peace knowing there will be days

I won't be ok.

Heart Beat
Journal entry - 4.2017

I woke up to heart palpitations. As I click the button on my new heart monitor, the significance of the heart dawns on me. The heart is the beat, the life force of our bodies, but that's not all. Our heart defines us, allows us to feel, give, and receive love. Love. What more powerful force is there? The heart holds both physical and metaphysical significance. My heart has been broken both physically and emotionally, yet still I am strong. I am a passionate soul. I wear my heart on my sleeve. Makes sense that out of all of the side effects, my heart would suffer the most. I have multiple pains that no one should have to endure at one time. Yet I am here. My heart still beats, slowly, yet the rhythm still flows. It takes courage to continue to love with a broken heart. Love in every form. Not just romantic. It takes courage to live life daily and love life knowing that any time the beat may stop. The dance may be over. But I can not focus on that. If I share my heart with you, please be kind to it. Be patient with me. Be still with me. Know that I am healing and choosing to have you in my life, but please remember I am fragile. I don't want to question intentions. I want to be free. Every heartbeat is a sign of the gratitude I have for my life. That alone is worth a thousand smiles. I am a woman of immaculate strength... my heart, body and mind heal more and more each day. The other side will be incredible. I look forward to dance to the rhythm of my future

Living in love

I am making room for love while diving into my healing. Ever since I got out of the hospital a feeling of New has come over me. I can't Really explain it. I don't want to sound cliche and say the near death experience "woke" me up, but in a way it has. I feel light, free and beautiful.. This is not to say I won't have bad days but I am making a conscious effort to find the good and live in the presence of love. Yes, I still have pain, yes I am still sick and tired , yes I am still fighting cancer, but Yes I am still here. I am blessed to wake up, make Ginger Tea and listen to my beloved Coltrane. I am blessed to be able to taste the sweetest mango while sitting on the balcony listening to the birds sing. I am blessed. What will wake you up? Find your reason to live in love, then continue to grow there.

The Decision

Pain is always around the corner so hold space for healing;

don't let fear, pain or ego stop you from living your best life.

I have experienced enough pain and negativity for a thousand souls. Trust me. Happiness and love are conscious decisions, but once the decision has been made watch all the glory you will receive.

Cacti

After my morning meditation, the theme for the day is protection. I recently realized that I am extremely vulnerable. It's a radical act to allow yourself to be truly open to yourself and others. With that comes a lot. At times I am bombarded with false promises and dreams. I believe people, and their words. I am extremely sensitive now. I have no time to feel any more pain than that which I already do on a regular basis. Promises of love, care, friendship, time, have all been made and not all have been kept. Visions of Cacti came to me this morning. A cactus is a survivor, it prevails in the harshest temperatures and remains physically strong at all times. It has a protective exterior yet is made of water and is soft on the inside. It's beauty is questionable at times but just when you think it has nothing to offer, it can give birth to a beautiful flower.

Affirmation: There is nothing wrong with protecting myself. Warriors have shields. I can be vulnerable, lucid, loving and still shelter my Spirit. I must preserve my physical sanctuary, my sacred space.

With every Breath

At times the world may feel heavy. Feels like one big sick joke. You may feel as if it doesn't make sense. You may feel lost, stressed , confused and hurt at times, and that is ok. It's ok to wander in the unknown. It's ok to cry so hard your Spirit shakes. It's ok. Hold on to the truth. Hold on knowing everything is done with Divine timing. Remember, with every breath you take you are moving forward, every breath you are getting through and surviving . Be kind to yourself. Calm waters are ahead. It will get better

Ghosts

Today I am haunted. Haunted by the words of my ex lover.

He broke up with me days before my cancer diagnosis in 2016. I had gone through many tests and we knew a result that could possibly be life changing was coming. Before that could happen, he felt that ending our relationship was best. We remained living with one another, until physically and financially I couldn't do it anymore. The whole " I still want to be your friend" while in a whole other relationship, a month after our breakup, was just too much. I was getting sicker and sicker fast! Our mental health has a huge impact on our physical health, and being in so much emotional pain was sending me to an early grave. I couldn't allow those emotions to have such ownership of my life. I moved from my beloved Harlem back to Los Angeles to be with my family, a move that would save my life, I hoped. Still, ever so often I was haunted by his words. He felt no one would consciously choose to be with someone battling cancer. "Who would choose this?" "Who wants this, no one", it was just too hard. I didn't realize how impactful his words would be until, fast forward to my most recent relationship, and as this one crumbled, I thought, he was right… no one really wants me. No one wants the woman with cancer. The burden is too heavy to carry. I felt unworthy due to my disease, so once again I put up with another relationship where I gave more than my partner. I felt grateful to another person just for caring about me. The bare minimum. Ultimately, he would almost shatter my Spirit. I try to hold on to the truth that I am enough, but it's hard. Even as I am haunted by his words, and a second heartbreak, a voice inside of me screams "choose yourself." Now is the time to choose myself. This is the lesson. This is the truth. This is what will set me free.

Release

I cried because it felt good,

it felt human,

it felt free

Self

If you love something, fight for it.

Stage II.
Pushing through.

Words to self

My body is remarkable and resilient

Speak power into your cells

When you are ill, tell yourself you are healed.

You are not weak

Look at everything you have been through

It takes strength to still be standing

You are shedding what no longer serves you in order to regenerate into your new form

You are power

you are a warrior

you will survive.

Pep-Rally

I woke up this morning, stood in the mirror and gave myself a pep-talk.

The woman looking back was terrified.

I told her it was going to be ok.

she believed her (self)

Canvas

I am truly a piece of art. Seeing what my body and mind can handle is remarkable. I have a thousand emotions all laid out like colors on a canvas. I cry not because I am not strong, but because I am aware enough to accept and deal with my emotions. I wear my tears and pain like a silk slip on sun-kissed skin. Graceful. I can not hide my hurt like many do, my pain breaks free intensely, like a John Coltrane solo. I am beautiful. I love hard. I am an open book. You are witnessing the rise of a woman whose healing is being painted right in front of your eyes.

Armour

Do not turn away from your battle.

Suit up

Fight it

Anyone can join an army

But it takes a strong Spirit to become a Warrior.

Freedom
Journal entry - 5.2017

Have you been holding on to something you need to let go of?

Easier said than done, but LET IT GO. It took months for me to grasp that concept, but damn I feel so free right now! Some shit ain't worth holding on to. Especially if it's detrimental to your health.

Holding on to pain, anxiety, expectation, doubt, fear, or a person, can literally manifest into physical health issues. At my weakest point I realized half of what I was going through was emotional, and I needed to let things go, forgive the situation, and continue with my healing.

This release and let go...I forgive you shit, just happened about a week ago.... Lol. Trust me it was not easy... I hold no pain, anger or hatred in my heart... I no longer question my self worth... I'm free!

Will there be days where the "Devil" will sneak up with your favorite flowers and candy, romanticizing your fears? YES..!

It's ok to have bad days but don't dwell in them. I am learning two major lessons in this cancer and heartbreak journey, patience and forgiveness:

Patience comes with time and forgiveness is a conscious decision.

Niaje Adah

Fever

Last night was hard… I lost consciousness.

Salt Water graced my cheek as I woke up in my mothers arms. She was wiping HER tears off of MY face. I told her everything would be ok. She called me her Warrior baby...her little light beam. Look at God, look at how many chances I have been given to survive. I am light. I now see and truly believe that I wouldn't be here today without this mindset. My baby sister told me I am surviving solely because of my love for life. I believe her. Knowing the power of our inner light in any situation is key. Accept your power, your grace, your beauty, and shine. See yourself as a light that radiates and impacts not only the positive in your own life, but for others as well. I see my light. I own my light. I live in my light. Do not let anything take your light for too long...power up and press through...day after day I continue to fight for my light with my light. May it never be extinguished again ! I see Me. I see You.

Pathway

... there will always be obstacles. Find your light. Light your way.

The Lesson

Challenges are proven to make one stronger and wiser.

one must be willing to acknowledge them as lessons, not loss

Affirmation: I am gaining ever more knowledge of my true self through these challenges.

Marathon

Every morning that i wake up, i am closer to victory

Tribe

The only people I desire in my life are the ones who value me in theirs, especially when I have nothing else to offer but my flesh, bone & spirit.

Security

The first person you think to call in the midst of a breakdown.

Caterpillar
Journal entry - 6.2017

Every once in a while I look through old pictures. Doing so can bring up many emotions. Usually I look at pictures of the pre-cancerous Niaje, but this time I chose the deathly ill Niaje: 80 pounds, sunken face, dark under eye circles, wearing diapers, could barely walk without a cane Niaje... whew! I used to hate this Niaje. I looked at her and felt disgusted. She was sick, hurt and suicidal. She felt unloved, betrayed by her lover and her God. I really couldn't understand why all this was happening! What was my Karma? Now when I look at her I see the strongest most beautiful woman ever. She got me through to this point. She never gave up. She fought fear with faith. She is still fighting. Funny it was easier looking deathly ill. People could see my battle. They could understand it. Now that I've gained some weight and appear to be "better" , it's harder. Imagine looking in the mirror and appearing to be "normal" yet still running fevers, having heart issues and living the same pain as when looking deathly ill. It went from " you don't look that bad" to "you don't look sick", both piercing my heart with the harsh reality that I'm still fighting this disease. I have to hold on to the strength I had a few months ago. I need it now more than ever. As I prepare for another round of chemo I pray to hold on to the appearance and energy I have gained these past few weeks. I pray my body remains strong. I am prepared for disappointment, but I try to affirm success in my treatment. I'm so thankful to have come out of the depths of hell. Nothing seems as bad as that anymore. I've literally died and was resurrected, so there is nothing else to fear, right? Thankful for the journey. Grateful for my Spirit. Yes, I will still cry my eyes out tonight... release any fear I still have inside. Going in for treatment is still scary AF.

Watching God.

At times she couldn't SEE but she remained faithful. Less than a year ago I was told I had 15 months to live... 15 months! Hearing those words sent me into a deep depression. Still I fought. Even when I felt I had no more to give, I fought. Words hold power and I truly believe in the Power of the Mind. You know that corny phrase "if you believe you can achieve", well that shit is true. Now I'm not saying that I can magically heal myself, but I have magically been healing myself. I'm doing a hell of a lot better than 6 months ago. My friend Mir told me to "Go Crazy" and believe in the magic, miracles & manifestations so much, that now I truly believe it is real, that I am healed. So that's what I am going to do. Who knows the future? I am riding a roller coaster with my hands up at every dip, but I know one thing, I will NEVER lose. To my cancer fighters out there, even in death we do not lose! Warriors don't die. So fear not. Enjoy the moments, live now and believe in YOUR miracle. Everyone's path is different. Walk in your truth.

I got this

Anyone else like always being in control? Ok, well I had a rude awakening over the past year. I Lost control of damn near everything in my life. Lost my health, my love, my lifestyle, my money, my friends, what I thought (keyword-thought) was everything. To say I was humbled is an understatement. After losing everything it took me months to believe that I now have everything to gain. What I thought I had control over was actually an illusion. Everything will be what it is supposed to be. Life is one long on-going lesson. You better pass the class exam or that same class will hold you back for the rest of your life. I am closing chapters and actually learning from them. I now feel freer than I have ever felt. We can't control the future. Prepare and plan yes, but stay present. If you still feel the need to control shit... control your thoughts, your energy, your Spirit, and what you put out into the Universe.

Master The Moment

Woke up and jumped straight into meditation. I had one of those nights where my mind races a mile a minute and I start to think about life after cancer. What am I going to do? How am I going to get there? What if? Laaaawd it just wouldn't stop. Anxiety is a crazy thing, and I really have to fight my mind in order to release it. It's hard staying present and living in the moment. The past and the future are like ocean currents dancing with the seashore of the present. Sometimes that dance feels like a riptide. You will get to the shore eventually, you know. Just remember that once dry sand is on your feet, you will still have to walk the rest of the journey ahead . So ride the waves to shore and save your energy.

Affirmation: I am exactly where I need to be.

I have done one hell of a job getting to this point

Doing my best
Journal entry - 9.2017

I am way too hard on myself. The closer I get to recovery the harder I am on me. At times I feel like a loser because I wonder if I should be doing more? I question if I am doing enough? So many people give me ideas. I should write a book, start a company, take classes, and use this 'free time". I start to feel a lot of pressure. I must remind myself I am healing. Yes, I have free time, but it ain't by choice. Cancer ain't filled with lounge days y'all. I am constantly fighting. Shit ain't easy. There are times when I sleep all day. There are days whereI find my mind can't seem to comprehend, let alone focus on anything. There are moments where I'm in so much pain my body just gives out. I'm doing my best, but even with that I feel guilty at times. I contemplate life after cancer and I start to get stressed out. Am I doing the work to prepare for that future? How will I sustain myself? I should be on my grind, my hustle, am I being left behind? Ugh! It's a lot. Everything is as it should be and it will fall into place I tell myself. My life is being led by the timing of the Divine. I am successful. I am in recovery. I am resting, I am reflecting, learning and becoming the greatest version of myself possible. I define my own success and with that

Niaje Adah

I will continue to live my life the best way I know how at this point. I Am Learning, Loving, and Letting go of comparison and expectation. It ain't easy though.

| **Comfort**

Never take for granted,

A fully belly,

A free mind &

A painless night.

A slice of Comfort & Joy
Rosemary, coconut banana bread

Wet ingredients:

- 1 1/3 cups mashed overripe bananas (3 large)
- 2 eggs or equal equivalent egg replacer (i use ground flaxseed)
- 1/3 cup plant-based milk (I use almond milk)
- 1/3 cup coconut oil, (melted w/ a sprig of rosemary)
- 2 tablespoons pure maple syrup**
- 2 teaspoons pure vanilla extract (I use mexican vanilla)

Dry ingredients:

- 1/2 cup brown sugar
- 1/2 cup rolled oats
- 1 teaspoon baking soda
- 1/2 teaspoon baking powder

- 1/2 teaspoon fine sea salt

- 1 1/2 cups baking flour

- 1 teaspoon Cinnamon

Crumble topping (optional)

- ¼ cup Coconut flakes, chopped walnuts, chopped rosemary.

- ½ cup flour

- ½ cup brown sugar

- 4 teaspoons softened vegan butter

- 1 teaspoon cinnamon

Directions:

1. Preheat the oven to 350°F (180°C). Lightly spray a 9x5-inch loaf pan with oil and set aside.

2. In a large bowl, mash the banana until almost smooth, and make sure you have 1 1/3 cups.

3. Stir the wet ingredients (egg/ground flax, milk, melted oil, maple syrup, and vanilla) into the banana until combined.

4. Stir the dry ingredients (sugar, oats, baking soda, baking powder, salt, cinnamon and flour) into the wet mixture, one by one, in the order listed. Stop stirring when there are no flour clumps at the bottom of the bowl.

5. Spoon the dough into the loaf pan and spread out evenly.

6. Combine all crumble toppings with flour and butter. Toppings should form into lumpy chunks.

7. Pour on top of loaf slightly pressing it down

8. Bake the loaf, uncovered, for 45 to 55 minutes (I bake for 46 to 48 minutes, but your time may vary), until lightly golden and firm on top . The top of the loaf should slowly spring back when touched. Insert a toothpick into the center, if it comes out dry, viola!

9. Let loaf cool for 30 minutes. Then, slide a knife around the loaf to loosen it and gently remove it from the pan, placing it directly onto the cooling rack until completely cooled

10. Slice the loaf once cooled.

11. Enjoy!

Listen & Learn

At times we are forced to slow down.

sit back and master inner mental / spiritual strength.

there are lessons to this

Quiet down

The answers are all there.

Niaje Adah

Silence

Instead of vocalizing my pain and hardships

today I will give gratitude to the ability to sit still.

#Choosejoy

Joy is a conscious decision.

We must constantly Choose to enjoy the present, remain in gratitude and accept the now.

It's all about perspective.

View

I'm now learning that everything is about perspective. Just because things may appear to be upside down, who is to say they aren't meant to be that way? Or hell, maybe they were always upside down and we are just now seeing it correctly. Whatever has flipped in your life, take it as a positive thing. Learn from it. You never know, your new vision may be opening doors to new dimensions of life, freedom and peace.

My mind is free so my feet can wander anywhere they choose.

| Tijuana

Learning to hold on to my spontaneous self. With everything going on, at times I don't feel like me. I'm normally a busy body, a 'miss do it all". The cancer has slowed me down tremendously. I never know how I will feel until the day of. A lot of my plans get cancelled. Thank God I have friends who are patient and continue to treat me like I'm "normal". They push my limits and do things that will make my heart and Spirit happy, even if that means driving three hours to take a picture with a donkey in Tijuana, Mexico!

Tribe 2.0

There will be times when you need others.

Choose wisely.

Surround yourself with those who See your light, enhance your Spirit and Feed your Soul.

| Entrepreneur

In a world where people ask "what do you do" as a first question, I say I'm fighting Cancer. My reality now is this is a full-time Job. I traded the office for the hospital. It's stressful, time consuming, and a bit overwhelming... sounds like a job to me... only now the gains are higher and I feel more accomplished when even the little goals I set are met. I'm literally working to stay alive. Working for myself. I'll tell you one thing though, don't ever take a lunch BREAK for granted. Working w/ cancer is a rare occurrence, I mean the whole having an appetite is one thing, but a break in general is hard to come across...but yea...that's what the fuck I'm doing.

Alien
journal entry - 1.2018

Over the past couple months I've gained more and more strength. I've finally gotten into a groove with my treatments and I can say I'm starting to live a little more stable. With that comes being more social again. Call me crazy but I don't relate to people like I used to. Life is just different now. I do not judge, for we all are on our own path, but, my outlook is far beyond the average. I've been through too much, seen too much. I'm super sensitive to energy now. I can't fake it anymore, if it's not for me I can't be around it. Funny enough, I may come off as shy or antisocial, but I always meet whoever I'm supposed to, and oddly enough they're always the people others glorify, whether based on fame or social status. My tribe is small, but I don't have to question their intentions, and that is worth more than gold to me. Lately I've had a pit in my stomach, something feels off. Someone is off. The truth will reveal itself in due time, until then, if I allow you in my force field, just know it's genuine. I don't have time or space for anything else.

The Groove

Life is about cumulative "start-overs." It seems whenever I get into a groove my body crashes and boom, I must start all over again! Each time, I grow stronger and wiser. Each time, I'm force fed a lesson I was meant to digest. Today I am grateful to have a bit of energy, to be back home, back to creativity, real food and another day to ultimately do whatever I choose.

Blessed to be able to always start over.

Niaje Adah

Trust

God is here

Cultivate

Burn it to the ground.

Fear will not grow here

Growth

Like the seed, I have survived the deep dark soil. I have fought and grown to penetrate out of it's depths. I shall rise towards the Sun and bloom as the most beautiful flowering form of myself. A sweet smell will linger to remind me of my victory. A beautiful bouquet made of miracles, gratitude and strength. I look beyond the clouds, patiently waiting, aggressively fighting until my day to blossom.

Seeds

Be careful what you feed your soul. Recognize your Power.

The mind is unbelievably strong and will grow whatever seeds we may plant therein

Affirmation:

I am planting the seeds of a fruitful abundant life.

Negativity no longer lives in my body.

Niaje Adah

Resurrection
Journal entry - 4.2018

Today, on this Easter Sunday, I awoke to a text from my nurse. It read:

" this time last year we almost lost you, but you fought through. I hope you hold the Spirit of this resurrection Sunday, and Dr. King with you. Our fighter, you keep rising. Celebrate today"

April 1 2017, I went into the hospital to prep for surgery to remove another tumor. Funny, I was nervous as all hell. Scared shitless really. I was overly weak, and had been having heart issues. My mom gave me a kiss and the longest stare into my eyes. Nothing was said. A picture was taken before surgery on April 3rd and that's all I remember. I woke up 3 days later from an induced coma attached to what looked like a thousand machines. I fell back "asleep" and woke up the next day, beyond drugged, I could barely speak, I was in the ICU.

I later found out my heart had actually stopped on April 3rd. While in surgery my organs started to bleed. This caused stress on my heart after surgery, and it stopped beating for a few seconds.

Thank God I don't remember the scary part. I remember the kind nurses, and my family and friends who sat with me day after day for over 2 weeks. I was released on Easter Sunday 2017.

I say all this to say, you ever look back on your life and say, like damn, I've been through some shit! Yea, and guess what? You made it! You walked through the tunnel of darkness day after the day and yet... you always moved towards the light! Survival is the light! My nurse's text is so much more than words. The fact that she mentioned resurrection Sunday and Dr. King hit me so hard. This past Sunday was Easter and today marks the 50th anniversary of Dr. MLK's assassination. So yes, I will continue to resurrect and fight. Yes, I fight with grace but know the fight is not easy. The work is physical, mental and spiritual. The darkness will always come, but we must always choose to keep walking, crawl if we have to, towards the Light. Let's just keep moving forward, even when we have doubts.

Niaje Adah

Grounded

Never sit in fear,

Always stand in faith

Birth Month

May. What used to be such a joyous month is now filled with so many emotional triggers for me. May 2016 changed my life. Although I do not dwell in the past, I still have remnants of trauma that rise up and steer me off course. I got diagnosed, dumped, and dangerously depressed all within a three week span of time. My whole life got flipped upside down and it all happened in May, which is ironically my birth month. After receiving news this past Monday that I now have cancer nodules in both lungs, it seems as if May has yet to redeem itself. So yeah, needless to say the past three days I have been in super spiritual mode. Not only is my world heavy, but the world around us all seems to be heavy, and as the empath that I am, ya girl can't take it. So what do I do? I'm constantly speaking positive affirmations, meditating, having conversations with God, and holding on to what is true for me. I'm releasing what no longer serves me or my greater good. I made sure to schedule a therapy session this week, and I went to my support group last week to help keep shit in perspective. With everything I have gone through, I still manage to acknowledge a light within me. I am grateful and truly blessed to still be here. That alone is worth celebrating. This

Niaje Adah

is not the life I thought I would be living, but it's the life that I got, for now anyway. That is my focus. There were nights when I was so sick, so heartbroken, I thought for sure I wouldn't wake up. I had to live and experience that pain to get to where I am today. Everything is temporary, with that we must learn to identify our triggers so we can protect our Spirit on the days when this life feels a little too permanent. We must learn to break out from what is ultimately unreal and focus on the real. I've learned to have compassion for myself. I have been buried in darkness and I have dug myself out. My past has made me who I am today. Although May is a constant reminder of when my life "fell apart", I now know it came UNDONE in order to be put back together, stronger. Life Itself is the greatest University. In order to live our best lives we must truly be willing to listen, learn, and do the necessary work. To forget is a false realm. Forgive your past. Flourish in your future.

The Taurus

I never once thought I needed to "find myself". If life is a journey and our experiences are lessons, then simply put, we must continue to learn. Do not confuse transition with being "lost". We must all do the internal work, some more than others. I'm proud to say that I am Magic. Who I am now, and who I will continue to grow into is fu*king amazing. It wasn't easy to get to this point, and it ain't always easy trusting my magic. Still, I'm shouting to the Universe, "I'm here," and I'm authentically living MY truth. Lost is a state of mind. I choose to believe my God will never allow me to wander without guidance. We have all been given the tools. We must make the conscious decision to use them!

Brave

With everything I have been through I still believe in love. I've learned to love myself during this process more than I could ever imagine. I'm focused on my health now, but when the timing is right I will love again, and the right man will enter my life. He will be a conscious lover, intelligent, driven, and in tune with his emotions. We will lift one another up and walk through this journey of life together as one powerful force. I am me, he is he... two divine souls who will choose to do the work and make it work.

Stage III.
Making it work.

You.

If Hallelujah had a heartbeat

It would belong to him

The One?
Journal entry - 4.2017

He showed up at my hospital bed . Showering me with flowers, hot tea and laughter. We spoke for hours upon end until visiting hours were over. He promised to come by tomorrow. I didn't scare him. My situation didn't turn him away. Dear God if he's not the one, please let this end quick and painless.

Fact

Affirmation: I am deserving of love, patience and honesty.

Niaje Adah

Stripped

I speak my truth. My transparency has gotten me through this battle. I will speak about whatever pain I feel until it makes its way somewhere else. I wasn't always this way. At times I took vulnerability for weakness. I would keep everything bottled inside. Trying to work it out alone . I was the rock. I was everyone else's rock. Well, when the shit hit the fan, like a rock, I started to sink fast, and the only way out was to be open & honest and let others carry me up for air. I no longer wanted to drown. I wanted to breathe. I started sharing my pain. The real shit I was dealing with everyday. I realized that the truth is a loving act. To be honest with myself and others was the most powerful I've ever felt. I now know that even on my darkest days acknowledging and being honest with myself is truly an essential life force.

| Abusive Relationship

Yesterday I spiraled down into a dark space. I was emotionally abusive to myself. There are times when the weight on my shoulders feels so heavy I collapse, hard. The constant obstacles become overwhelming. Self love turns into self hate. Negative affirmations of worthlessness crowd my brain. I'm in transition right now. No longer on my deathbed, yet still quite a ways away from where I would like to be. I feel burdened by my situation. At times it feels like I have nothing and that I am no one, when God knows I am blessed.

We can become blinded by our circumstances. Yesterday was a bad day. I haven't had one of those in a while, even when we know our triggers, our shields can't always protect us. I literally had to fight with myself to get back to sanity. Today, I awoke exhausted and drained. I cried long and hard off and on for hours. I tried to cleanse my body from toxic thoughts and feelings. I pray today will be better because I need strength. This week is treatment week. Physically I will get beat up, so there's no need for me to do it to myself, emotionally. I pray that God protects me from all thoughts that cause me harm. I affirm that I am a beautiful being worthy of love, and a peaceful and healthy life.

One day at a time...amen...

Thrive

Surviving, to me, is awareness.

Awareness of the negative and the positive, and making conscious decisions that serve my Spirit.

Spirit

Beyond the physical

I am worth healing

Damn.

Life can be fucked up and delightful all at once. The beauty is that we are always evolving, constantly changing, and hopefully growing wiser with each day.

Progress
Journal entry - 6.2018

I had surgery Monday and the bull-headed Taurus in me wants recovery at lightning speed. My biggest lesson throughout this journey has been patience. I've gotten a lot better. I don't pressure myself as much, I'm learning to go with the flow. I've been waiting to have this surgery for over a year. It represents tremendous progress. No big tumors, and the cells throughout my body, have decreased by nearly half! Radical remission is near! So yeah, naturally when we see the finish line we want to sprint ahead right? Well I've learned that everything truly happens when it is supposed to. As long as I have the finish line in view, I know I will cross it. Like my mama says "you're already a winner", meaning that the only race we are running is against ourselves. Once you truly understand that, you can give yourself a break. Be kind to yourself and own the fact that you are doing one hell of a job!

| Red Flags

The truth will always come to light. Have you ever had a feeling, a thought, a situation that you tried to ignore? Like a truth you may not want to hear or face? If I've learned anything about 2018 it's that this year ain't sugar coating shit! There has been a lot of loss, a lot of pain and uneasy emotions. On the other hand there has been more clarity than ever. I see things for what they truly are. I am being forced to. With that, I must fearlessly walk in my power. Not just me, but we as a conscious collective, are being forced to. Forced to be real, to be honest, to be true, to be passionate and fearless! There is no more time for darkness. Whenever I fall into the darkness, I have to break away and power up through the mind. I have to reinforce the greatness within myself. I am beautiful, I am worthy of love and life!! It's not easy. We owe it to ourselves to gain the consciousness that knows that despite all circumstances, the light is always there.

Vision

No degree of darkness can extinguish the glow of this soul's inner light

Stir the pot

Instagram entry - 7.2018

What happens to a dream deferred?

You hold a dream close to your heart, affirm it, then watch it manifest when the time is right. A lot of hard work and prayer got me to this moment in time. This has been a dream of mine for years, I just never knew when it would happen. The thought of potentially dying and having disease rob me of my life had me shook up!!! I have so many goals, dreams and visions that I want to live to see manifest! I took a leap of faith. As soon as I physically could, I enrolled in Culinary School. Yes, you heard right. me, Niaje, with Stage IV cancer, officially became a culinary arts student! I figured it was now or never. Shit, I died and resurrected for a reason, I figured. Time to manifest some dreams… if I could do it, so can YOU!

Believe •Affirm •Manifest.

New Life

Growth, at times, can definitely feel more like a shit show than a celebration.

Agape

Woke up feeling abundantly loved. No specific reason, person, or act, just the knowing that everything difficult I have experienced, God has seen me through. We must remember that we are all loved, because we ARE love, created from the image of the highest form of love itSelf.

Seen

He told me I am more beautiful now than ever, and I believed him. Not that I need validation but with everything I've been through and all the hard work I've done, my internal light is finally radiating out.

Home

Your smile is my sanctuary

Your eyes are my altar

| **Bondage**
Journal entry - 9.2018

How much more can one person go through?

Why is it everytime I start to feel free, I get shackled again?

What part of the lesson am I missing? What or who do I need to release?

God give me strength, I don't think I can take much more, I'm just so exhausted.

Time out

At times you will feel helpless. Some shit is simply out of your control.

There is power in knowing you can't fix everything.

It's called faith.

Affirmation: I am open and trust the process

Christmas Day
-A text to my Mother

Today was divinely orchestrated!

I wish you were here!

I love you Mommy

The day after Christmas

At exactly 10:09 am

Four text messages would knock the air out of my lungs

and change my world forever.

The beginning to our end.

I woke up the day after Christmas to an uneasy partner. Something had changed. The energy was different. It was dark. His energy was off. I didn't know exactly what had happened, but It felt ominous. I wasn't going to allow anyone to try and steal my lover's light, so I reminded him of his beauty & power, the essence of his true being. I was trying to uplift his Spirit. I offered to make us a hot cup of tea.

I walk down the wooden steps of his parents' home, to the kitchen. With every creak of the stairs, my heart sank. I began reciting affirmations of love, a daily practice, but something felt different. A pit grew in my stomach. I felt unsettled. I brought my cell phone downstairs with me this morning, a first on this trip. I made our tea, put on his favorite sitcom, and waited for him to come downstairs. My phone goes off, I try to ignore it, but something compelled me to check it. I open my phone only to see the words

"I'm sorry... I can't handle this anymore".

My heart sank. I ran up the stairs straight to the bathroom, no one was there. I open his bedroom door but I can't find him. My heart begins racing. I couldn't speak, but I mustered enough strength to whisper out "baby" numerous times to no return. I went back into his room and everything became a blur, I opened the door to his closet...

The spirit of God took over me. My hands and body anointed with strength only the almighty could give me, I managed to get him down. With only my bare hands and God's grace he fell to the floor. We both cried out, I dropped to my knees gasping for air. Sobbing out only silence because there were no sounds, nor words, that would come. The man I loved has just attempted to end his life, knowing I would be the one to find him. My world completely shattered. Never would we be the same.

A Shoulder

Oh GOD, help me.

I come to you on bruised knees and palms facing the sun

I am leaning into the divine and screaming out for help

What can i do?

How can i undo this pain, trauma and fear

Pray for strength

Pray for sanity.

Pray for light.

I surrender!

Blemish

Weeks after the incident a shift occurred, a distance, a stain was left on me.

I became a reflection of the secret, a witness to it. A reflection of the reality we couldn't bury and act like never happened. Over the next few months I would pour immeasurable love into this man, while carrying our secret around like a heavy backpack. I was depleting my energy to make him stronger, all the while the stronger he got, the more distant we would become. My love, support & loyalty was not enough, this experience had changed us forever. As much as I tried not to believe it, I knew he would leave eventually. I knew he would find someone whose mere existence didn't remind him of pain and trauma.

A fresh start. A new beginning. A new season? Whatever.

I just needed him to survive, I needed him here.

I needed him to know he is loved.

Depression

We hide ourselves from others in plain sight.

Healing

Remember, what we choose to see in the dark is not real. It is solely a glimpse of the lesson to be learned. It is the light that carries the truth.

Focus

What have you gone through to make it to today?

You survived.

You are here.

Niaje Adah

Chef

If only you knew what it took for me to get to this moment in time. The past couple of months alone would have taken even the strongest warrior out, yet here I am. I didn't want to make completing my culinary program a big deal. My mother reminded me it is a big deal, and why this moment is actually so huge.

Fall 2016 chemo caused the paralysis in my digestive system. I couldn't eat, I now had a feeding tube and was on a liquid diet for nearly 5 months. I lost over 40 pounds. I was now given just 15 months to live, only to survive, and survive, and survive. Never would I have imagined I would still be standing here, let alone attending a culinary arts program. It's crazy how fearless one can become when faced with death.

Don't wait to pursue your dreams, face your fears NOW. You owe it to yourself. I could have been like, I'm still in treatment, I'm too sick, and still in pain. I could have dropped out in January when my world felt so heavy, but there was that little voice, that little light, telling me I could do it. Trust in God. Trust in You. Keep pushing through, even when it feels impossible. It will get hard, but the reward, that feeling of accomplishment, will be well worth it!

| For You, For Me

I wonder if you know

how truly phenomenal you are.

The world needs you.

Hussle & Boog

The bond between twin flames is a sacred one. It is an alchemical marriage of the highest order. Souls connect ON purpose WITH purpose. Emotional, physical, karmic, spiritual, all of the above. Soulmate relationships can be the magical energy of transformation and creation with a partner you consciously choose to experience life with. Never by chance we are sent to one another, it is always for a reason. A lesson curated by the universe and with divine timing, but many will never experience this type of bond. You attract what your energy vibrates to, but sadly too many fail to understand their own energy, which may actually prevent one from realizing such a blessed union. I say all this because two beautiful souls found each other. Two souls made a conscious decision to experience life , transform life, ex. grow, learn, experience and create life ex. raise children together. Even after the physical, there's a bond that can never break. Intentions so true never fade, they remain solid. Blessed to have been a witness.

April 2019

Attachment

This soil is not rich enough for you,

plant your seeds elsewhere.

You deserve fertile ground

Remission
Journal entry - 7.19.2019

Three years, one month and seventeen days. That's how long I prayed for this moment. When I reflect on my cancer journey it now feels like an out of body experience. The amount of pain and suffering I endured no one should feel in one lifetime. How did I survive? How did I get here? I'm still in shock, still processing it all. Wednesday I had a day where I let it all out. I cried like a newborn baby, a cry so deep and heavy it rocked the ancestors. I needed that cry. I needed to know it was ok. That yes I am here and yes I am finally in REMISSION!

I was a survivor before the remission diagnosis. I am a Warrior. Even when I felt I couldn't keep going, I did. I remained vulnerable, yet brave. Gentle, yet powerful, faithful and honest. That's what got me through. That's what kept me alive. To be transparent even when it doesn't look or feel good. Now, I know this journey isn't over, it's actually just beginning. Now I just want to sit in gratitude, bathe in thanks, and give the glory to GOD.

We read of miracles in ancient texts, but how often do we realize they still happen everyday, and right in front of us? Keep believing in your miracle. It may not happen when/how you want or expect it to, but it will happen when and how it's supposed to.

Re-birth

I went from simply surviving to relearning how to live

Enough

Comparing my life with other people, or situations will kill everything that is meant for me. I know this, yet I am human, so at times I fall short on self love and belief. I have been granted a new life. I must remember that when the darkness creeps in, spreading vicious lies, I am on my own time, a seraphic time. I will surround myself with those who support, inspire and uplift me in this new journey I now embarc on. I deserve success in all aspects of my life.

Affirmation: I am worthy of patience, love and loyalty. I am beautiful, intelligent, compassionate and ENOUGH.... a trillion times over

Prosperity

Success for me now is being true to myself, and allowing the world to see me as this un-perfect person. The transition is not easy and it's extremely painful. I still have a lot of work to do, but I am easier on myself now.

New Normal

Lately I've been trying to balance a LOT, too much in fact. So now i've thrown myself completely off balance, experiencing total exhaustion to put it mildly, trying to be superwoman. Adjusting to my new normal is not easy. There is so much unsaid about life after cancer. This shit is hard! Two months into remission and I'm handling a job, planning my career, taking care of my injured mother, trying to be an attentive partner, and maintaining a social life! All of this while still going through withdrawal from years of medication and now receiving maintenance treatments. I'm suffering from the physical, mental and spiritual after effects of cancer from the past 3 years.

My first maintenance treatment was bittersweet. I sat in the infusion chair and I became extremely irritated. Like, why can't I just magically be all better? Like poof! Bye cancer, bye side effects, it's time to get back to normal. This is only the beginning of a new journey. I may need treatments for the rest of my life. I may have fatigue for the rest of my life. I may have memory, lung and heart damage for the rest of my life, BUT I am here. I AM HERE. With that mantra, I take a few breaths. Inhale acceptance and release expectation. I wasn't supposed to be here now, so I'm already winning. Everything else is just icing on the cake.

What expectations are holding you hostage? How do you adjust yourself back into focus when things get cloudy?

Affirmation: I am here.

Baby Steps

Remember, wherever you are right now is a lot further from where you were. Whether you feel like you are taking steps backward or forward, trust the journey. You will end up exactly where you need to be. I feel extremely blessed to be in remission. With that I also have to remember recovery is a long road ahead, patience.

The side effects of treatment have left me with extremely weak and with very fragile lungs. My heart has also been affected in ways that may never be reversible. Lately, I've been on the go, so when my lungs began to hurt I didn't think much of it. I have some sort of pain literally everyday. I went to the ER yesterday and was told I had a bacterial infection. I was in shock.

Crazy thing is, a couple months ago, a year ago, this type of infection would have taken me out! So yes, I am still in a fragile state, but look how far my immune system has come! My cells are actually fighting back, trying to keep me strong! I was given antibiotics, fluids, vitamins, a bed rest order, and after a few hours I was sent home! Home! They would have kept my ass a few months back!! So Yes, it's frustrating but it's also reassuring that God got me! That I am here for a reason.

Niaje Adah

As I lay with a heating pad on my chest, drinking a nasty herbal concoction, I can only be filled with gratitude. I'm 3 months into remission and already I am so much stronger. I'm not where I want to be but I am overjoyed with where I am.

Cloud 9

I pray to be as fluid as a cloud.

Always moving in the right direction

trusting the path blindly, fearlessly floating forward

even in its stillness it's secretly moving.

Abundantly onward

Summer Cherub -2019

At 6 weeks I felt my greatest wish leave my body and drain out on the bathroom floor. I truly still do not have the words but if writing is my therapy then I hope to purge out this pain I carry inside of me.

Imagine how it would feel if doctors told you it would be very difficult to conceive a child, only to become pregnant! I was both excited and terrified after receiving my test results. I remember praying and talking to the Spirit of my unborn child. I remember begging that it stay healthy and come to full term because I'm scared daddy will leave me if I am defective, infertile. Now here I am, having just miscarried, and feeling more concerned with my partner not wanting me, then processing what had just happened.

And, like I feared, although he tried his best to console me, when it was time for him to leave, he walked away and I knew things would never be the same. This would add on to the list of fears and reasons why I feel unworthy, a list, the lover before him gave me. I'm still haunted by my previous lovers' words, "that no one wants to deal with all of this", who would consciously choose this? No One.

Cancer has managed to affect every aspect of my life. Add fertility issues to the list.

I buried my angel baby deep down inside. I wiped away the tears and wore a smile because I didn't need anything else to burden anyone else with.

Distance

Although near,

you feel far away

Why do I feel so unworthy?

I give you my all and still,

It never feels enough.

Tomorrow

Time moves slow as molasses

when you await

The sweetest future

Healing Chai Tea

Ingredients

- 5 cups water
- 3 inches fresh ginger, sliced into coins
- 2 cinnamon sticks
- 3 star anise
- 1 tablespoon black or pink peppercorns
- 60 cardamom pods
- 20 whole cloves
- 1 teaspoon whole coriander (optional)
- 1 orange peel (optional)
- 1/2 cup whole leaf loose black tea or 12 tea bags
- 3/4 cup honey, more or less to taste
- 1 tablespoon molasses
- 1 1/2 tablespoons vanilla extract
- 1 tablespoon fresh lemon juice

Instructions

1. Place the water, ginger, cinnamon, star anise, peppercorns, cardamom, cloves, coriander, and orange peel in a wide saucepan and bring to a boil. Reduce heat to medium-low and simmer for 20-30 minutes.

2. Remove from heat and add in the tea. Let steep for 7-9 minutes, then strain the entire mixture through a fine sieve into a large bowl. Stir in the honey, molasses, vanilla, and lemon juice, then pour into a mason jar or other airtight storage container and store in the refrigerator for up to 1 week. (Alternatively, the concentrate may be frozen for up to six months.

To serve

1. Serve with milk of choice (i love oat milk) in a ratio of 1:1.

2. To serve hot, heat 1/2 cup chai concentrate with 1/2 cup milk thoroughly

3. To serve cold, add milk and chai to glass filled with ice, stir thoroughly

4. Blend it, add to smoothies, shakes, baked goods recipes!

5. Enjoy!

Open Palm Sunday
Journal entry - December 29, 2019

As I look down at my hands I think about all I have been through. My hands have held thousands of prayers, wiped numerous tears, have hurt and helped others, have saved a human life and have even held an object to take my own.

The past couple of weeks I have been going through it. At times I couldn't believe I prayed for this. I prayed for life. More time. I am learning how to live again. How to love again. With living comes all of life's problems. I'm physically, mentally, and financially stressed. Niaje is rebuilding and it's not easy. I had a breakdown! You know you're grown when you have to pay for your own rehabilitation. Like, no one is going to save me? That was the realization. I have to save myself. Love myself, despite what others may think, do or say. I have to do the work to heal and accept all that I am, all the God potential within me. It's not easy! So many of us are faking the work, barely touching the surface and getting by. It's so much easier to be ignorant, but I wasn't given a second chance at life to just settle with getting by. I seriously contemplated taking my own life after how many years of praying for restoration? Whew! Depression is real. Triggers are real.

I felt physically unattractive, comparing myself to every healthy attractive girl on instagram. I felt inferior because I didn't have a successful career. I felt less than because I couldn't afford a flourishing lifestyle like so many around me. I felt hurt & once again abandoned. but most of all I felt unworthy after the loss of my child; when in actuality I am chosen, highly gifted and was given a second chance at life. As you can see I was blinded by lies and insecurities I fed myself and insecurities others projected on me. The thing about the journey is that through it all I never gave up. I may have crashed at times, but I always picked myself up. Who's to say I won't fall again, but I now know I am triumphant. I am the light even in darkness! I release all that was and welcome all that will be. Amen

And so it is...

So many chapters are being written. So many chapters are closing. God will determine my end. Knowing that, I remain grateful and surrender.

Stage IV.
Hard to believe, Hardly giving up.

New Year Affirmation.

I am deserving of the same Love, Loyalty and Energy I give to others.

Intuition

half-loved.

by him.

by me.

Commitment

Every once in a while a love so deep shall occur. Usually such love does not come easy. It is then that those lovers must make a decision to withstand the current and wait for calm waters, or break into the waves and crash onto separate shores. Being forced to crash onto a separate sandy beach, bruised and broken, is not easy but I will survive.

In case you forget- Affirmations

I give thanks simply for waking up this morning.

Fearlessly, I trust in my Creator .

I walk through life knowing I am highly favored and made with intention

I am a vessel of abundance.

Never shall I take this life for granted.

For my Thrivers
journal entry - 2.13.2020

This week I met up with a group of Black women each of whom was recently diagnosed with Cancer. One thing I tried not to do is focus on their fears. I never got into the support group community. I found (in my experience) a lot of the ones available to me were groups of people wading in their pain and fear. I hated being around people all focused on the negative. I would always feel so depleted and depressed afterwards. I wanted to feel a sense of hope and encouragement, so I wanted to shift that narrative. Yes, we need support and a safe space, but at what cost? We should uplift one another, fill each-other up with possibilities. Help each other think differently and build hope together. We should speak our fears, feel them, give them space and then release them. Sadness and trauma compromise the immune system, and when fighting cancer you need every ounce of strength you have. It's not easy, but we have to keep living the best of our abilities. Keep laughing, surround yourself with loved ones, go out when you have the energy to, eat fresh colorful foods and give yourself space when you need to rest. I kept emphasizing life and living to these groups, speaking about regular ass shit so these women could feel some sense of normalcy. Cancer or not we have to protect our energy. At the end of one meetup, a woman called me her favorite "inspiration-er" because she never feels "influenced", only compelled to be Herself. She was her own motivation, she said, but she was inspired by me, my energy and my truth, I was floored. I swear everyday Spirit is pushing me in the right direction. I just want us all to know WE are our own Source. Everything is inside of us already. We all deserve to know that. A wholistic approach. To bring ourselves back to WHOLENESS. If "the highest human act is to inspire," then I am extremely honored and grateful to hold the title, "Inspiration-er".

The Healer

Listen to your body, it will tell you everything you need to know

Listen to your Spirit, it will validate all that you already know

Deja Vu

How many times can a heart break? I guess however many times it takes... for what? Unfortunately, I don't have the answers. All I know is that my heart has been breaking repeatedly the last few years. Yet still I am standing and it still beats. Now don't get me wrong, there has been joy and love in between the breaks, but I have been fighting heart pain nonstop for years. I prayed endlessly for calm waters. I wanted time to just wade, relax and take everything in. My waters have not been calm for more than a few days, more like weeks at a time. This time the waves have crashed so hard, I've ended up on shore so battered that I question God. Not why, but how? How will I get through this again when I am so exhausted? Questioning why is almost pointless. There is no real reason as to why someone may get sick, perish or endure turmoil. Simply, we learn from the experience. Hopefully we grow and continue on our journey.

When diagnosed with cancer one goes into survival mode. When in "remission" you go from simply surviving, to learning how to live again. Throughout it all there is a little whisper, a fear. What if the cancer comes back? With every new scan your mind fights the worst anxiety imaginable, and when you get good news your whole body rejoices. 2020 has been interesting to say the least. My feet have yet to be planted on stable ground. I've been receiving blow after blow. We lost Kobe Bryant. The man I loved decided to end our relationship, and a hospital stay revealed my biggest fear had come true. The cancer was back!

Darkness is quick to move in. I've been haunted with feelings of unworthiness. Am I worthy of life? Love? Happiness? The darkness tells me no. I'm haunted by words a man told me almost 4 years ago, when I was first diagnosed. He said no one would sign up to be with me (while fighting cancer) because it's just too hard. Times like these I feel he was right. Still, I tried to be brave, and love again. I wanted to believe in love. So I did, and I'm still in love. I'm haunted by the words of my first doctor saying my cancer would never go away. Now here I am, 6 months into remission, with recurrence. So yes, I am disappointed and heartbroken right now. I need space to process. I need help holding up because I am weak and I will fall. They say God only gives us what we can handle, so I try not to question my fate, but this feels like one sick joke. Deja Vu. I tell myself I am a true warrior, I will dust off my armour and prepare for this fight again, but I need time to sort through this pain, in order to get back to my healing.

Niaje Adah

Poppy Field Reflections

As I sit in a field of poppies, surrounded by such colorful, endless beauty, my mind drifts back, every so often to my anxiety. Tomorrow I embark on yet another journey, another battle. Tomorrow I will start round one of a new immunotherapy treatment.

I never thought I would be in this space again. I feel a sense of betrayal, but from who, God? My body? The universe? I think I have asked why a million times. I have questioned everything in me as to why, and if for some reason, I am the one to blame. Fact is, there is no one/nothing to blame. Simply, these are the cards I have been dealt and just like the last battle, I can choose to fight or give up.

Am I tired? Yes. I do not have the same fight in me I once had. I will have to dig deep and extract an immense amount of strength, mentally, emotionally and physically to get me through. Crazy, these pandemic days are challenging times for everyone. I still can't believe, that on top of everything else, fighting cancer is back on my list

Feeling worthy is at an all time low. It's hard to feel whole when your heart is broken in so many ways. I really just want to live life without the burden of cancer clinging to me. Sigh, just when I thought life was getting back to "normal" , this is happening again.

Super-bloom

Like the Poppy I will continue to blossom every year regardless of circumstances

Like the Sun I will illuminate & radiate new life

May 8th, 2020

I give thanks to the Creator for another year.

Despite it all I continue to continue

Blessed to Be

Happy Birthday Niaje, I'm so damn proud of you

Broken Up-ish

Not together

Not apart

Not serving my Spirit.

Peace & Acceptance

Death, it is a certainty for everyone. Thank goodness not many have to deal with its reality so soon. As a warrior diagnosed with stage IV cancer, the conversation about death happens quite often. Yes, we fight and we want to stay alive, but the Creator has the final say. I have flatlined, suffered a heart attack and have spent many a night in the ICU, but never have I felt as close to death as I do right now. I can honestly say, as I write this, I was preparing to go.

After days in the hospital alone, I was finally allowed a visitor. My sister friend sat at my bedside, looked into my tired eyes, and said, "It's ok". Fighting off tears, she wanted me to know it was ok if i wanted to go. She could see the suffering on my face, she could feel my agony. She had witnessed cancer's wrath firsthand when her beloved Nana passed away. We sat and had the most beautiful conversation about what may be the inevitable. Warriors fight for self, but they also fight for their loved ones. The thought of my loved ones grieving my transition weighed heavy on my fragile mind and body. The heaviest weight I felt was in thinking of my mother. She had already lost her eldest child, my sister. I carried the guilt of my sickness like it was a new born baby. I couldn't leave her alone. Another sister- friend told me, " if you are ready, then i am ready, but I really feel you have more time".

As the days went by in the hospital, one by one I made sure to share my thoughts, my peace, with all those who had supported and genuinely loved me. One by one, my seemingly empty cup filled up. The fear of death was stripped away from me by the understanding, compassion, empathy and unwavering unconditional love of so many. They understood this was not goodbye but a beautiful see you later, How grateful I am to have a tribe that truly Sees me. After everything was said and done, I was finally at peace. I surrendered.

Warriors

If my story is to end soon, please do not say I lost the fight. Warriors can not lose a fight, especially one they didn't choose to be in. So in that case we are winners because champions are those who despite their back being against a wall, despite having no choice, they suit up, shielded with strength, dignity and faith, to fight the unknown. Warriors are victorious

Niaje Adah

In Peace-
written from my hospital bed, July, 13, 2020

When I think about my life I'm at peace knowing I did my best.

I consider myself a genuine person. A good person. People like myself are hard to come across, and sadly many of the real ones experience real pain throughout our lives.

I was never perfect, but I hope anyone who has ever gotten a chance to know me felt my love.

I love hard and I'm loyal. I believe in those I love like no other. Whether rooting for your dreams, never letting you doubt yourself, or constantly reminding you of your worth, I hope you know I love you.

None of us know when our time to go will be. As I sit in the hospital I know that if I were to pass tomorrow my life was not in vain.

My Godfather, Michael Beckwith told me I came to the Earth to help and to heal others. To be a light. He says my words, my knowledge and transparency have given strength and hope to so many others. He says I've helped fuel many fights for many people to win their own battles.

When it comes to love I know I was sent here to show unconditional love to those who ultimately were not strong enough to love me.

I have received many messages from people thanking me for sharing my story. My truth. That me, Niaje is an inspiration & motivation for so many. I am beyond humbled.

But honestly, I do believe, as far as right now, that my greatest achievement in life has been no short of a miracle. To literally save a human being with my bare hands. If that is why I came to this Earth, to save just that one life, then I have done my job. I have fulfilled my purpose.

I've attended one of the best universities, been successful in my career, went to culinary school, had a home, and built a family of close friends who have never left my side.

I have traveled the world, danced until the lights came on, drank endless amounts of wine and laughed until my belly hurt. I have made amazing meals, fed strangers and brought lovers together.

I am proud of who I am. I am loving, caring, loyal, funny, silly, smart af, spiritually tapped in and overall a wonderful person.

Niaje Adah

My story right now may be filled with pain, loss, and at times a sense of unworthiness, but I know that those conditions are not who I am.

I am tired right now, but I am not giving up.

At the moment I feel shattered, but that gives me the opportunity to put the pieces of me together and create something new.

For those who have given up on me. It's their loss. I hold nothing but love.

To those who continue to breathe life and love into me I am eternally grateful, and I hope you feel that. I love you.

It may not be in the cards for me to have someone to love me unconditionally, to have children or even to grow old, but I am proud of everything I am right now.

Remember to be kind to yourselves. Look at everything you have survived and feel good that you are still here. You should feel proud. If you need to work on something, do it now, don't procrastinate! Hold yourself accountable. Hold your friends/fam accountable. We can't keep hurting ourselves and others. Let's do better. We are in a time of healing. Distractions no longer will do. You deserve better

Phased Out

People are transient, like the phases of the Moon

Find the Souls who truly love unconditionally

Who will rise with you every morning like the Sun

Our End

His eyes turned blank as he told me he was starting a new season. I felt as if my heart had officially disintegrated.
"Is this what broken feels like?"
I lay there, now knowing for sure that the only man I have ever possibly dreamt to do life with, was moving on.

I felt disposable...again.

To feel both unworthy of the Creator and now my lover was all too much.

I had no more fight to give.

He could start a new life, and mine?

I would start to not only ideate my own death,
but grieve a person who still was very much alive.

Defeated

I cant believe i'm going through this shit again.

Deeply

And Still, I loved him.

He gave me life in more ways than one

and unconsciously in return, i saved his.

Wound

I tried to hurt you, I wanted you to feel the same pain that i felt.

Agony will make a person do crazy shit!

I am not built to inflict pain

I only ended up hurting myself

Shattered

I feel closer to the other side; It's as if I'm living between two worlds. One is of the physical realm and one is of the Spiritual realm. In order to survive, I'm learning to surrender. To accept the fact that I am presently at rock bottom, feeling broken, shattered. At the moment, I feel I am that woman who through it all, wears pain elegantly like a lace gown. I've learned another great lesson, that being broken and on the bottom can indeed be a powerful position because the only way to go now, is up, but you gotta get up. To repair and rebuild that which is broken. There is nothing negative or shameful about admitting your at your lowest point. Breakdowns are a part of life. This is where you fully let God in. This is The Breakthrough Opportunity.

This current temporary cycle is teaching me to not be hard, but to be gentle and kind. I unshackled myself from the expectation of being a "Strength Muse". I screamed, I cried, and wailed day after day on bruised knees for my ancestors' guidance. I found the true meaning of strength. The power to surrender. To sit still & listen. I'm forgiving myself for things I've done while dwelling in the bottom. I wanted him to feel pain too, but it didn't sit right in my heart. That isn't part of my character, so I owned up to my darkness. Hurt people hurt people as they say, and I fell victim to the darkness's lies.

I'm learning that rejection can actually be protection, and that God never punishes or abandons It's children. It is we who fall short, forgetting our spiritual practices. In order for my full healing to take place, not only do I have to blindly trust God, but I must trust and believe in myself as well. We all possess the power of the Creator within us. We are made in God's likeness and image. I can heal myself fully by acknowledging the power of the Almighty within me.!

Awaiting : Reborn

The laying of hands I needed were my own.

I stretched out my arms to the heavens and released every inch of pain

I held myself tight yet gently like a mother with her newborn child

For Me

To all the hearts I tended to

The ones that had no intention of caring for mine

I forgive you

Daddy Issues

I tortured myself days on end

Thinking I wasn't good enough

That I lacked value because of my circumstances

I am not incomplete

Because I couldn't give him what he was missing

Hard Truth

Abandonment created room for Abundance

Courage

I once told myself I would never fall in love again.

but, I did, and I fell deep.

With every ounce of my soul.

Despite the outcome,

I am proud of my heart.

FYI:

Everything ain't always good. Some people feel if they put on a front of happiness everything will be ok. Well guess what? That doesn't work. Living with a disease and heartbreak is not easy, but it has taught me a lot. I'm now extremely truthful with myself. I've learned to accept who I am in each moment of my life. We are human beings. We have emotions out the ass and that's ok. I'm not always going to be happy and inspired. Some days I'm gonna cry and be depressed. Other days I will be angry and question my faith. To feel is ok. To feel is to accept the present and learn. We can not truly live our best lives if we do not accept ourselves. Also, we can't live our best lives if we do not accept others for who they are.

Allow people to feel. Internalizing emotions can manifest into all sorts of ailments. That's why I share my emotions. I am true to myself, therefore I can free myself from all the heaviness. Emotion is a scary word to a lot of people. Emotions/Feelings. So many children, especially little black/brown children grow up thinking that showing certain emotions, like fear or pain, make them weak. The thought of being weak in many people's minds leaves them to only acknowledge the emotions of anger or happiness.

Niaje Adah

Well guess what? Baby, you are an ocean of emotions and it's ok to feel every wave that comes. Feel, and once you do, turn within and use emotion as a stepping stone to living authentically in your glory.

I am who I am because fear, sadness, joy and happiness continue to teach me who they are. No matter how low how high I may get, I always come back to the middle ground to continue to fight for my life. Fighting for life isn't just about having a disease or hardship to get through, it's about doing the work in order to live whole and feel fulfilled. We all deserve a whole, complete life, not one stunted by the stigma of unacknowledged feelings.

Inheritance

Their Pain & Trauma is not your burden to carry

Release and Let go.

Niaje Adah

Fall

There is freedom in letting go. Today I woke up amongst the trees and mountains and felt free, not because I didn't have any more pain but because I was no longer controlled by it. As I looked out my window I saw all the beautiful gold color leaves across the porch, and then I noticed the bare limbs of the trees swinging across the horizon. I thought to myself how even the trees have to let go of their leaves every year. The trees themselves shed the dead leaves and await the new birth in the spring. So like the trees, no longer will I hold on to what is not alive, instead I look forward to what will be. The promise of tomorrow. The freedom of seeing the beauty in the now, while having hope in the future.

I see the beauty in accepting myself in all forms and for all seasons. I understand the power of getting through another season of perseverance and determination. As my leaves turn golden I realize the infinite possibilities I possess within myself. I stand here naked like a majestic maple-tree. Naked, yet armed with faith, dignity, strength and grace. I release, I let go, I move forward. I am grateful for my past as it has got me to where I am today. I release myself from the shackles of my pain. I am now free to live again. New leaves await me, actually a whole new tree .

Open

With honesty comes wisdom.

There is power in truth

Especially when speaking to self.

Accountability
Journal entry November, 2020

Growth & wellness without accountability is a sham.

You are lying to yourself if you believe you can progressively move forward without holding yourself accountable to your past

Yes, we all possess the ability to become better individuals, but there is a lot of work to be done on the journey.

A lot of folk bury their past, then plant roses on top of the soil.

Heavy rains will come, and when they do, are you prepared to clean up what you have been trying to hide, what floats to the surface?

There are many tools to aid in our healing. The first step is awareness of self. So many use therapy, meditation, & self-care as a shield, some as a crutch. Some are not truly doing the work, but blocking the work they need to do out of fear or self-delusion.

To project happiness does not reflect healing. Healing is a mix of all emotions and until you are ready to feel them all, sadly you are just swimming in circles.

You can not run from your past whether it be today , tomorrow or 20 years from now. Your past WILL catch up with you in your process completely healing.

So be honest with yourself on your healing journey. Be honest about your mistakes and wrong doings. Apologize to those you've hurt. Be authentic. Most importantly forgive yourself and let go of any guilt.

You can only run for so long. So you might want to trade those track shoes in for crocs. The journey is constant. Might as well get comfortable.

Unconditional

And still, I pray for you.

Despite it all, you still own deep space in my heart.

The Journey

Time is the greatest gift of compassion I can give to myself, for if I believe tomorrow will come then I can affirm that the life I am living today is not in vain.

| Grace

I am allowed to feel grief and gratitude.

There is room for both.

Rest
Coconut Curried butternut squash soup

Ingredients

1 Tbsp coconut or avocado oil

2 medium shallots (thinly diced)

2 cloves garlic, minced (2 cloves yield ~1 Tbsp)

6 cups peeled & chopped butternut squash (1 small butternut squash yields ~6 cups)

sea salt + black pepper to taste

2 Tbsp curry powder

¼ tsp cumin

1/4 tsp ground cinnamon

1 14-ounce can coconut milk

2 cups vegetable broth (DIY or store-bought)

1-3 Tbsp maple syrup (or sub honey/agave)

1-2 tsp jamican hot pepper sauce (sriracha,is fine)

½ cup chopped Cilantro(optional)

Instructions

1. Heat a large pot over medium heat.

2. Once hot, add oil, shallots, and garlic. Sauté for 2 minutes, stirring frequently.

3. Add butternut squash and season with salt, pepper, curry powder,cumin and ground cinnamon. Stir to coat. Then cover and cook for 4 minutes, stirring occasionally.

4. Add coconut milk, vegetable broth, maple syrup and chili garlic paste. Bring to a low boil over medium heat and then reduce heat to low, cover, and simmer for 15 minutes or until butternut squash is fork tender.

5. Use an immersion blender, or transfer soup to a blender, and purée on high until creamy and smooth. If using a blender, return soup back to the pot.

6. Taste and adjust seasonings, adding more curry powder, salt, or sweetener as needed. Continue cooking for a few more minutes over medium heat.

7. Serve as is or with garnishes of choice. I love cilantro and extra chili paste.

8. Store leftovers covered in the refrigerator for 3-4 days or in the freezer up to 1 month. Best when fresh.

9. enjoy!

Deep Breath

You may not be where you would like

But look how far you have come

Embrace all that you have accomplished to survive

Give thanks to the many lessons you have learned throughout the journey

When it all starts to feel a little too heavy

Rest

Lean into your loved ones

Dive into your faith,

You deserve to relax, to release and to just ride the waves of life

Wherever they may take you.

Invocation

"Help" without expectation of outcome is a prayer within itself.

Stage V.
Still standing : Surrender.

Favor

I am grounded in deep love and deep faith

at the core of my existence, perseverance runs through my veins

look how eloquently I have survived

triumph is on the other side of this storm

Prayer & Praise

I am in need and in plenty.

With a grateful heart I rejoice in the very breath used to speak of my sorrows

Through it all I trust that the work of Spirit is taking place

With faith I affirm

All will be exactly as it is meant to be.

I and I

You don't need anything to be spiritual. You don't need to denounce religion. You don't need sage or crystals, you don't need candles or full Moons. Those are simply tools to help/enhance the journey. In fact those tools will not work unless you understand the truth. The truth is that you need to be aligned with THE Spirit. YOUR Spirit. YOU. You already have a direct connection to whichever higher power you believe in. You are the essence of that power. Jesus sat on a mountaintop. Buddha sat under a tree alone, with nothing but themselves, and a direct connection and understanding of their oneness with GOD. Ain't enough smudge in the world that can guide you to your purpose and favor, if your connection is blocked. Intuition is our higher voice. It's inside of you first. Everything else is secondary. We must realize we are one with our Creator, made in Its likeness and image, a manifestation of It, then we will understand that everything is energy and has purpose…

With that realization, watch how your vision clears, weight is lifted off you, and doors begin to open up. It's all about awareness … consciousness.

Niaje Adah

The Cycle

Fear not when your petals begin to fall

You will bloom, over and over again

Authenticity

What does the truth feel like?

-Healing

| **Honestly**

Joy is our birthright

THE Affirmation

I Am

Healed, Whole & Complete.

In the meantime

I never thought I would be writing this in real time, present time. I had always thought by the time I got to tell my story It would have some magical, mystical ending. Cancer-Free, endless joy, a healed heart you know ? Instead, I'm writing this while still in active treatment, with healing still in progress. One morning I woke up and realized this is the part of the journey where I need the most help. The in between time.

This is the space where the breakthroughs happen. This is the time of purging the emotional cancers I hold within, in order to regain my health. Not only do I need to share how I became cancer-free or found love, God is demanding me to speak the truth. My body and heart had failed me again, I hit the bottom hard and yet here I am, still sharing how I walked through the darkest valley, blindly trusting Spirit to guide me to higher ground.

So here we are, a collection of words that document my ups and downs, and how despite it all, I've managed to make it through.

Healing is constant. We are in a state of perpetual restoration. That is the journey. With that we must give ourselves and others continuous empathy and compassion. If you have ever felt the pain of a broken heart, you are a Survivor. Have you ever fallen on the floor, in tears, praying for help? Did you get back up? That makes you a Warrior. If you've ever had a night when you felt so ill you thought you might not wake up to see another morning , but you did, then you are a Champion. With everything I have been through, I now know for sure that I Am made with intention. We are here for a reason and we owe it to ourselves to continue to fight for our light. I've learned that joy does indeed come in the morning. With every breath, we manage to shine. With every breath we are enough, as we are.I may not know what tomorrow will bring, but i have learned to give myself grace. To be kind to myself, and trust everything will fall into place as it is meant to be. None of my Pain will be in vain, therefore I surrender and continue to fight diligently to live a life I deserve. A life of the infinite possibilities and blessings because I am worthy.

I like to think of us all as broken in some way. We walk through our lives, and with every experience, we put pieces of ourselves together, creating who we are becoming day by day. By the end of our journey, I like to think we have become complete. So with that, remember

Niaje Adah

If you fall apart, no matter how many times, no matter what happens, try again. You can always rebuild. So, when you begin to feel less then , or unworthy, remember to stand in your power and affirm your wholeness. You owe it to yourself because you are worthy, you are perfect, whole and complete.

Possession

I spent a lot of time

waiting for a miracle

not realizing

the miracle already resides in me

i am a miracle.

Niaje Adah

Now

I decided to set myself free

And just like that, my life changed.

Behold

Defeat became deliverance.

Claim it

I am ready to receive my blessings.

For me, For us

You are loved.

Put Pen to paper

∽

The next few pages are for you. Write down Takeaways from my story. Write down and release an experience from your own journey. Write what feels right. Writing saved my life. You have a story to tell. Let it out.

Connect Further with Niaje Adah

Instagram: @niaje

Twitter: @naturallyniaje

Website: bricksandhoney.com

www.ingramcontent.com/pod-product-compliance
Lightning Source LLC
Chambersburg PA
CBHW022055290426
44109CB00014B/1109